KETO FAT BOMBS COOKBOOK

Easy to Follow Keto Friendly Recipe Cookbook for Beginners

(Easy Tasty Keto Recipes of Snacks and Treats Recipes)

Edwin Brabham

Published by Sharon Lohan

© Edwin Brabham

All Rights Reserved

Keto Fat Bombs Cookbook: Easy to Follow Keto Friendly Recipe Cookbook for Beginners (Easy Tasty Keto Recipes of Snacks and Treats Recipes)

ISBN 978-1-990334-17-7

All rights reserved. No part of this guide may be reproduced in any form without permission in writing from the publisher except in the case of brief quotations embodied in critical articles or reviews.

Legal & Disclaimer

The information contained in this book is not designed to replace or take the place of any form of medicine or professional medical advice. The information in this book has been provided for educational and entertainment purposes only.

The information contained in this book has been compiled from sources deemed reliable, and it is accurate to the best of the Author's knowledge; however, the Author cannot guarantee its accuracy and validity and cannot be held liable for any errors or omissions. Changes are periodically made to this book. You must consult your doctor or get professional medical advice before using any of the suggested remedies, techniques, or information in this book.

Table of contents

Part 1 1
Introduction 2
About the Sweet Keto Fat Bombs 3
1. Hazelnuts and Orange Taste Fat Bombs 8
2. Chocolate and Pistachio Nuts Fat Bombs 10
3. Chocolate and Coconut Fat Bombs 12
4. Walnuts and Pine Nuts Fat Bombs 14
5. Cherry Taste Fat Bombs 16
6. Peanut Butter and Coconut Fat Bombs 18
7. Macadamia and Strawberries Fat Bombs 20
8. Chocolate Raspberries Fat Bombs 22
9. Chocolate Butter and Coconut Fat Bombs 25
10. Almonds and Hazelnuts Fat Bombs 27
11. Coconut and Pumpkin Fat Bombs 29
12. Sweet Frozen Berries Fat Bombs 31
13. Blackcurrants and Coconuts Fat Bombs 33
14. Strawberries Fat Bombs 35
15. Dark Chocolate and Almonds Fat Bombs 37
16. Cashews and Vanilla Fat Bombs 39
17. Hot Cayenne and Chili Peppers Fat Bombs 41

18. Peanuts and Coconuts Bricks Fat Bombs 43

19. Pistachio and Coconuts Fat Bombs 45

20. Choco Almonds-Coconut Butter Fat Bombs 47

21. Sweet Pine Nuts Fat Bombs 49

22. Fresh Raspberries Fat Bombs 52

23. Peanuts Fat Bombs 54

24. Milk Chocolate and Strawberries Fat Bombs 56

25. Nuts Fat Bombs 58

26. Lemon Taste Fat Bombs 60

27. Raspberries Fat Bombs 62

28. Dark Chocolate Fat Bombs 64

29. Blueberries Choco Fat Bombs 66

30. Wild Dried Berries Fat Bombs 68

Conclusion 70

Part 2 71

Introduction 72

Chapter 1: The Ketogenic Diet 74

What is Ketosis? 75

Benefits of the ketogenic diet: 77

A complete keto food guide 79

Chapter 2: Fat Bombs 86

Chapter 3: Sweet Fat Bomb Recipes 92

Keto Chocolate Coconut Candies 92

Neapolitan Fat Bombs 94

Keto Coconut Fat Bombs 96

Lemon Fat Bombs 98

Vanilla Fat Bombs 100

Chocolate Peanut Butter Fat Bombs 102

Red Velvet Fat Bombs 104

Almond Pistachio Fat Bombs 106

Espresso Fat Bombs 108

Peanut Butter Chocolate Chip Fat Bombs 110

Coconut & Almond Fat Bombs 112

Pumpkin Spice Fat Bombs 114

Berries and Cream Fat Bombs 116

Raspberry, Chocolate, and Coconut Bark 118

Keto Macaroon Fat Bombs 120

Keto Chocolate Fat Bombs 122

Chocolate Peanut Butter Balls 124

Walnut Muffin Fat Bombs 126

Cinnamon Fat Bombs 128

Keto Orange Fat Bites 130

Blueberry Fat Bombs 132

Cream Cheese Jello Balls 134

Almond Cookie Fat Bombs 136

Lemon Coconut Fat Bombs 138

Lemony Cream Cheese Bombshells ... 140

Frozen Butter Rum Chocolate Fat Bombs ... 142

Peppermint Fat Bombs ... 144

Pistachio Fat Bombs ... 146

Raspberry Fat Bombs ... 148

Mixed Berries Cheesecake Fat Bomb ... 150

Pecan Fudge ... 152

Chapter 4: Savory Fat Bombs ... 154

Smoked Mackerel Fat Bombs ... 155

Bacon and Eggs Fat Bombs ... 157

Bacon and Guacamole Fat Bombs ... 159

Pizza Fat Bombs ... 161

Jalapeño Pepper Fat Bombs ... 162

Bacon and Chicken Liver Fat Bombs ... 164

Salmon and Dill Fat Bombs ... 166

Sesame Fat Bombs ... 168

Beef and Cheese Meatballs ... 170

Cheesy Jalapeno Fat Bombs ... 172

Avocado and Eggs Fat Bombs ... 174

Savory Salmon Fat Bombs ... 176

Cheesy Pesto Fat Bombs ... 178

Pork Belly Fat Bombs ... 180

Veggie and Cheese Fat Bombs ... 182

Avocado, Macadamia, and Prosciutto Fat Bombs 184

Bacon Maple Pancake Balls 186

Barbecue Balls 188

Conclusion 190

Part 1

Introduction

This cookbook contains delicious and mouthwatering sweet ketogenic fat bomb desserts that are low in carb, but high in fat and contain mainly natural sweeteners such as stevia instead of white or brown sugars. The main reason why sweet keto fat bombs are the best solution for you if you want to eat something sweet, but still healthy is that there is no need to deprive yourself of delicious sweet things if your goal is to lose weight or simply maintain the good condition of your body.

That is why the sweet keto fat bomb recipes from this cookbook are the perfect solution for people who love sweet things, but don't want to consume tons of unhealthy candies, chocolates, sweets, pastry etc.

Many people that use a ketogenic fat bombs diet include sweet keto fat bombs as a part of their fat bombs or keto diets because sweet keto bombs are very simple and fast to prepare and offer an easy way to keep control over the nutrients and portions you eat.

Enjoy a collection of 30 delicious sweet keto fat bomb recipes from this cookbook while you work towards your health goals. Moreover, I would like to encourage you to experiment with the sweet keto desserts from this cookbook, adding your own flavors and tastes!

About the Sweet Keto Fat Bombs

What are the Sweet Keto Fat Bombs?
Keto fat bombs have low and medium amounts of proteins, low amounts of carbs, but a high content of fats. The same applies to the sweet keto fat bombs, except for the fact that they use different fats such as unsalted butter, chocolate butter, cocoa butter, coconut butter, and coconut oil and that they taste sweet.

Sweet fat bombs are small snacks that make an excellent source of energy for those who are on a low-carb diet and want to eat something sweet but with a high level of healthy fats. Sweet fat bombs don't contain unhealthy sugars, such as white or brown. What is more, sweet keto bombs don't contain honey or products with honey. Instead, the keto sweet bombs contain various sweeteners – stevia, monk fruit, and others.

The main advantage of the sweet keto fat bombs is that they contain simple ingredients that you can buy online or in every corner shop and can be prepared very fast. Moreover, it is easy to maintain control over the nutrients and sweet bombs portions you eat every day. If you are busy during the day, and you don't have time to prepare something healthy and sweet for yourself, but you want to eat healthy sweet things and follow the ketogenic path at the same time, then the sweet keto fat bombs would be an ideal solution for you. You can always have a few of the sweet keto fat bombs in your bag and quickly get out of a bad mood by popping one or two sweet bombs in your mouth!

Main Characteristics of the Sweet Keto Fat Bombs

- Low carb, high healthy fat (coconut oil, coconut butter etc.)
- Small balls or mini muffins size
- Sweet taste
- No sugar, contain only sweeteners – stevia in drops, powder or liquid format, erythritol, xylitol, monk fruit etc.
- No honey
- Stored in the refrigerator, baked, cooked
- Contain nuts, seeds, oils
- Contain spices such as cinnamon, cardamom, vanilla
- Main ingredients: coconut oil, coconut butter, unsalted butter, chocolate butter, vanilla, cocoa powder, stevia, seeds, nuts

Kitchen Utensils That We Will Need to Prepare the Sweet Fat Bombs

To prepare the tasty and mouthwatering sweet keto fat bombs fast, you will need to have the right utensils in your kitchen. The following list of tools will help you prepare your sweet bomb desserts easier and faster.

Food Scale

The food scale is very important to cook tasty sweet fat bombs, because you can use it to measure any solid or liquid food, and it will always indicate the quantity of ingredients that you need for preparing the sweet fat bombs recipes. Moreover, you can use your food scale in combination with a diet app, and get all the data you need to eat more intelligently and reach your keto diet goals faster and more efficiently.

Food Processor or Blender

Having a food processor or blender is critical for preparing sweet fat bombs because it will help you to process, grind, pulse, and blend unsalted butter, coconut butter, coconut oil, cream, nuts etc.

Electric Hand Mixer

Using an electric hand mixer will save your time, energy and hands, especially when you are preparing fat bombs where you need to combine various ingredients such as pulsed berries or nuts with unsalted butter, coconut oil or cream cheese.

Paper Muffin Cups or Candy Cups

Paper muffin cups, candy cups, or silicone molds are crucial when preparing sweet keto fat bombs, because often you need to bake, to freeze, to store, or to place in the fridge for a long period of time, sometimes even overnight, all your sweet mixtures.

The following chapters contain delicious and mouthwatering sweet keto fat bomb recipes that will sweeten your keto diet days and will have your taste buds come to life!

1. Hazelnuts and Orange Taste Fat Bombs

Preparation time: 25 minutes

Cooking time: 0 minutes

Servings: 10

Ingredients:
- 7 oz ground hazelnuts
- 2 teaspoons orange zest, minced
- 5 oz dark chocolate
- 4 oz coconut oil
- 20 drops of stevia
- cinnamon

- spray cream

Instructions:

1. Melt the dark chocolate in a double boiler for 15 minutes and mix in the other ingredients.
2. Pour the mixture into the small paper muffin cups or candy cups and place in the fridge for around 3 hours. Serve with the spray cream on top.

Nutrients per serving:

Total Carbs: 2.5g

Net Carbs: 1.8g

Total Fat: 9g

Protein: 2g

Calories: 74

2. Chocolate and Pistachio Nuts Fat Bombs

Preparation time: 25 minutes

Cooking time: 0 minutes

Servings: 10

Ingredients:

- 5 oz dark chocolate
- 8 oz coconut oil
- 8 oz cocoa powder
- 20 drops of stevia
- 4 oz coconut butter
- 1 cup pistachio nuts, ground
- vanilla
- sea salt

Instructions:

1. Melt the coconut oil in the microwave and combine it with the cocoa powder, vanilla, stevia, and salt.
2. Pour the mixture into the small paper muffin cups or silicone molds and place in the fridge for around 20 minutes.
3. Add half of a teaspoon of coconut butter into each silicone mold or paper muffin cup.
4. Melt the dark chocolate on low heat for around 10 minutes, stirring all the time.
5. Cool the mixture and slowly pour it over the fat bombs, adding ground pistachio nuts on top.
6. The fat bombs should be placed in the fridge for at least 4 hours.

Nutrients per serving:

Total Carbs: 2.8g

Net Carbs: 2g

Total Fat: 11g

Protein: 3g

Calories: 87

3. Chocolate and Coconut Fat Bombs

Preparation time: 20 minutes

Cooking time: 10 minutes

Servings: 15

Ingredients:

- 12 oz shredded coconut
- 6 oz coconut oil
- 8 oz cocoa butter
- cocoa powder
- 20 drops of stevia
- cinnamon
- spray cream

Instructions:

1. Preheat the oven to 330°- 350° Fahrenheit.
2. Toast the coconut for 10 minutes and then pulse using a blender.
3. Add the remaining ingredients except for the spray cream, place into a food processor and blend until smooth.
4. Pour the mixture into small paper muffin cups or candy cups and place in the fridge for around 3 hours. Serve with the spray cream on top.

Nutrients per serving:

Total Carbs: 2.3g

Net Carbs: 1.4g

Total Fat: 8.9g

Protein: 1.9g

Calories: 77

4. Walnuts and Pine Nuts Fat Bombs

Preparation time: 20 minutes

Cooking time: 0 minutes

Servings: 10

Ingredients:

- 5 oz walnuts
- 4 oz pine nuts
- 10 oz cottage cheese
- 5 oz unsalted butter
- 5 oz coconut oil
- 5 oz cocoa powder
- 20 drops of stevia
- vanilla

- cinnamon

Instructions:

1. Pulse 5 oz of the walnuts using a blender.
2. Melt the butter in a skillet, and then add in the cottage cheese.
3. Combine the walnuts, coconut oil, vanilla, cinnamon, stevia, cocoa powder in a bowl. Add the mixture to the melted butter and place in the fridge for 2 hours.
4. Form 10 fat bombs out of the mixture, add the pine nuts on top, and place in the fridge for around 4 hours.

Nutrients per serving:

Total Carbs: 6g

Net Carbs: 4g

Total Fat: 17g

Protein: 10g

Calories: 127

5. Cherry Taste Fat Bombs

Preparation time: 15 minutes

Cooking time: 0 minutes

Servings: 15

Ingredients:
- 2 oz fresh cherries
- 4 oz cherry syrup
- 8 oz coconut butter
- 4 oz coconut oil
- 5 oz cocoa powder
- 20 drops of stevia

- spray cream

Instructions:

1. In a bowl, add and mix coconut butter, coconut oil, cherry syrup, cocoa powder, and stevia.
2. Spoon the mixture into each small paper muffin cup, candy cup or silicone candy mold and place in the fridge for around 3 hours, serving with a cherry on top.

Nutrients per serving:

Total Carbs: 2.9g

Net Carbs: 1.5g

Total Fat: 11.8g

Protein: 3.9g

Calories: 69

6. Peanut Butter and Coconut Fat Bombs

Preparation time: 20 minutes

Cooking time: 0 minutes

Servings: 10

Ingredients:
- 5 oz peanut butter
- 6 oz coconut butter
- 6 oz coconut oil
- 8 tablespoons hulled hemp seeds
- 4 oz heavy cream
- 4 oz shredded coconut
- 2 oz dark chocolate
- 25 drops of stevia

- vanilla

Instructions:

1. Place all the ingredients except for the shredded coconut into a food processor and blend until they have a smooth and creamy consistency.
2. Melt the chocolate on a low heat, stirring for around 10 minutes.
3. Form 10 fat bombs out of the mixture and slowly pour the melted chocolate over the fat bombs, rolling the balls in the shredded coconut.
4. Cool and then freeze the peanut butter fat bombs for 50 minutes, and then you are free to serve them.

Nutrients per serving:

Total Carbs: 5g

Net Carbs: 3g

Total Fat: 21g

Protein: 10g

Calories: 179

7. Macadamia and Strawberries Fat Bombs

Preparation time: 25 minutes

Cooking time: 0 minutes

Servings: 15

Ingredients:

- 8 oz macadamia nuts
- 4 oz coconut oil
- 5 oz unsalted butter
- 2 oz cream cheese
- 1 tablespoon erythritol
- 15 drops of stevia
- 4 oz strawberries
- vanilla

- chocolate spray cream

Instructions:

1. Grind the macadamia nuts using a blender and mix them with the coconut oil and the unsalted butter.
2. Combine the macadamia mixture with the other ingredients, mashing with a fork.
3. Pour the mixture into each small paper muffin cup or candy cup and place in the fridge for around 3 hours, serving with the chocolate spray cream and the strawberries.

Nutrients per serving:

Total Carbs: 2.8g

Net Carbs: 1.9g

Total Fat: 15g

Protein: 6g

Calories: 99

8. Chocolate Raspberries Fat Bombs

Preparation time: 20 minutes

Cooking time: 0 minutes

Servings: 12

Ingredients:

- 8 oz raspberries
- 6 oz dark chocolate
- 2 oz cream cheese
- 5 oz coconut butter
- 2 oz unsalted butter
- 20 drops of stevia
- 2 tablespoons cocoa powder
- 1 tablespoon erythritol

- vanilla

Instructions:

1. Melt 6 oz of the dark chocolate in the microwave and pulse the raspberries using a blender.
2. Blend the cream cheese, unsalted butter, coconut butter, cocoa powder, stevia, melted chocolate, and vanilla using a food processor.
3. Combine the mixture with the pulsed raspberries in a mixing bowl, mashing with a fork, then place in the fridge for 2 hours.
4. Form 12 raspberry fat bombs out of the mixture and serve.

Nutrients per serving:

Total Carbs: 7g

Net Carbs: 4g

Total Fat: 22g

Protein: 12g

Calories: 159

9. Chocolate Butter and Coconut Fat Bombs

Preparation time: 20 minutes

Cooking time: 0 minutes

Servings: 10

Ingredients:

- 5 oz chocolate butter or hazelnut spread
- 5 oz coconut oil
- 4 oz heavy cream
- 20 drops of stevia
- chocolate spray cream

Instructions:

1. Place all the ingredients except for the spray cream into a food processor and blend until they have a smooth and creamy consistency.
2. Spoon the sweet mixture into the silicone molds or paper muffin cups and freeze for around 2 hours, serving with the chocolate spray cream on top.

Nutrients per serving:

Total Carbs: 4.8g

Net Carbs: 3.4g

Total Fat: 15g

Protein: 4g

Calories: 151

10. Almonds and Hazelnuts Fat Bombs

Preparation time: 25 minutes

Cooking time: 0 minutes

Servings: 10

Ingredients:

- 4 oz almonds
- 4 oz hazelnuts
- 15 oz cottage cheese
- 4 oz unsalted butter
- 2 oz coconut oil
- 20 drops of stevia
- vanilla
- cardamom

Instructions:

1. Melt the unsalted butter in a skillet and add the cottage cheese.
2. Pulse the hazelnuts using a blender and combine them with coconut oil, vanilla, stevia, except for the cardamom and the almonds. Add the mixture to the melted butter and the cottage cheese mixture and cool for 30 minutes.
3. Form 10 fat bombs out of the mixture, press the almond inside each ball and sprinkle cardamom on top.
4. Mixture should be placed in the fridge for around 2 hours.

Nutrients per serving:

Total Carbs: 10g

Net Carbs: 7.5g

Total Fat: 29g

Protein: 14g

Calories: 154

11. Coconut and Pumpkin Fat Bombs

Preparation time: 20 minutes

Cooking time: 0 minutes

Servings: 15

Ingredients:

- 10 oz pumpkin puree
- 5 oz cream cheese
- 4 oz coconut oil
- 2 oz coconut butter
- 4 oz almonds
- 1 tablespoon pumpkin-pie spice
- 20 drops of stevia
- 3/4 teaspoon ginger

Instructions:

1. Grind half of the almonds and melt the cream cheese adding the coconut oil with the coconut butter.
2. Mix all of your ingredients in a mixing bowl, pour the mixture into the silicone molds and press the almond inside each bomb.
3. Freeze the fat bombs for at least 3 hours and then you are free to serve them.

Nutrients per serving:

Total Carbs: 7.2g

Net Carbs: 4g

Total Fat: 16g

Protein: 6g

Calories: 88

12. Sweet Frozen Berries Fat Bombs

Preparation time: 20 minutes

Cooking time: 0 minutes

Servings: 12

Ingredients:

- 10 oz mixed berries, frozen
- 5 oz strawberry syrup
- 5 oz unsalted butter
- 10 oz cream cheese
- 15 drops of stevia
- vanilla
- cinnamon
- spray cream

Instructions:

1. Defrost the frozen berries mix in the microwave.
2. Place all the ingredients except for the spray cream into a food processor and blend until smooth and creamy consistency.
3. Pour the mixture into each small paper muffin cup, candy cup or silicone mold and freeze for overnight, serving with a spray cream and cinnamon on top.

Nutrients per serving:

Total Carbs: 8.9g

Net Carbs: 5g

Total Fat: 17g

Protein: 10g

Calories: 100

13. Blackcurrants and Coconuts Fat Bombs

Preparation time: 25 minutes

Cooking time: 0 minutes

Servings: 12

Ingredients:

- 15 oz fresh or frozen blackcurrants
- 8 oz coconut oil
- 5 oz coconut butter
- 10 drops of stevia
- 4 tablespoons monk fruit sweetener
- 2 oz dark chocolate
- vanilla

Instructions:

1. Defrost the frozen blackcurrants in the microwave if frozen.
2. Place all the ingredients except for the dark chocolate into a food processor and blend until they have a smooth and creamy consistency, and then freeze for 1 hour.
3. Form 12 fat bombs out of the mixture and melt the chocolate on a low heat, stirring for around 10 minutes.
4. Cool the dark chocolate and slowly pour over the blackcurrant fat bombs, then freeze the fat bombs for 1 hour and you are free to serve them.

Nutrients per serving:

Total Carbs: 8g

Net Carbs: 6g

Total Fat: 18g

Protein: 8g

Calories: 113

14. Strawberries Fat Bombs

***Preparation time:* 25 minutes**

***Cooking time:* 0 minutes**

***Servings:* 12**

Ingredients:

- 15 oz fresh or frozen strawberries
- 8 oz coconut oil
- 2 oz coconut butter
- 2 oz peanut butter
- 2 oz coconut flour
- 4 oz cocoa powder
- 10 drops of stevia
- 4 tablespoons monk fruit sweetener

- vanilla
- chocolate spray cream

Instructions:

1. Defrost the frozen strawberries in your microwave if frozen.
2. Place all the ingredients into a food processor and blend until they have a smooth and creamy consistency.
3. Spoon the sweet mixture into the silicone molds or paper muffin cups and freeze for around 2 hours serving with a chocolate spray cream on top.

Nutrients per serving:

Total Carbs: 9g

Net Carbs: 6g

Total Fat: 16g

Protein: 7g

Calories: 116

15. Dark Chocolate and Almonds Fat Bombs

Preparation time: 20 minutes

Cooking time: 10 minutes

Servings: 10

Ingredients:

- 7 oz dark chocolate
- 4 oz cocoa butter
- 4 oz unsalted butter
- 4 oz coconut oil
- 20 drops of stevia
- vanilla
- almonds
- chocolate spray cream

Instructions:

1. Melt together the dark chocolate and the cocoa butter in a double boiler for 10 minutes and mix with the other ingredients using a hand mixer.
2. Spoon the mixture into the silicone molds or paper muffin cups and place in the fridge for 4 hours.
3. Remove the fat bombs from the molds and serve with the chocolate spray cream and the almonds on top.

Nutrients per serving:

Total Carbs: 4g

Net Carbs: 3g

Total Fat: 19g

Protein: 5g

Calories: 129

16. Cashews and Vanilla Fat Bombs

Preparation time: 30 minutes

Cooking time: 50 minutes

Servings: 12

Ingredients:

- 4 cups of cashews
- 1 egg
- 1 cup flour
- 8 oz unsalted butter
- 1 tablespoon cream cheese
- 25 drops of stevia
- vanilla

Instructions:

1. Preheat the oven to 300°-320°Fahrenheit.
2. Toast the cashews in the oven for 10 minutes and then grind them using a blender.
3. Combine the cashews and all the remaining ingredients in a mixing bowl, using a hand mixer.
4. Make the crumbly dough, spoon the mixture into the silicone molds or candy cups and bake for 50 minutes at 300°- 320°Fahrenheit.
5. Cool the cashew fat bombs for around 2-3 hours and then you are free to serve them.

Nutrients per serving:

Total Carbs: 6.8g

Net Carbs: 3.4g

Total Fat: 14g

Protein: 6g

Calories: 61

17. Hot Cayenne and Chili Peppers Fat Bombs

Preparation time: 25 minutes

Cooking time: 0 minutes

Servings: 12

Ingredients:

- 8 oz dark unsweetened chocolate
- half teaspoon chili pepper
- half teaspoon cayenne pepper
- 8 oz cocoa butter
- 5 oz coconut oil
- vanilla

Instructions:

1. Melt the dark unsweetened chocolate in the microwave.

2. Melt the coconut oil and cocoa butter in a pan over low heat.
3. Add the chocolate, vanilla, chili pepper, cayenne pepper and mix all the ingredients.
4. Pour the mixture into 12 small paper muffin cups or candy cups and place in the fridge for around 5 hours.

Nutrients per serving:

Total Carbs: 9g

Net Carbs: 7g

Total Fat: 19g

Protein: 10g

Calories: 169

18. Peanuts and Coconuts Bricks Fat Bombs

Preparation time: *25 minutes*

Cooking time: *0 minutes*

Servings: *15*

Ingredients:

- 8 oz coconut butter
- 4 oz coconut oil
- 5 oz cocoa powder
- 8 oz peanut butter
- 4 oz raw or roasted peanuts
- 3 tablespoons erythritol
- 10 drops of stevia
- vanilla

- chocolate syrup

Instructions:

1. Combine the coconut butter with coconut oil, erythritol, cocoa powder, peanut butter, stevia, and vanilla in a mixing bowl, mashing with a fork until smooth.
2. Spoon the sweet mixture into silicone pan and spread it with a spatula.
3. Add the chocolate syrup, sprinkle with the peanuts on top and place in the fridge for 3 hours.

Nutrients per serving:

Total Carbs: 8g

Net Carbs: 6g

Total Fat: 16g

Protein: 9g

Calories: 149

19. Pistachio and Coconuts Fat Bombs

Preparation time: 25 minutes

Cooking time: 15 minutes

Servings: 12

Ingredients:

- 8 oz coconut oil
- 4 oz ground pistachio nuts
- 4 oz almond flour
- 4 egg whites
- 10 drops of stevia
- shredded coconut
- vanilla

Instructions:

1. Place the shredded coconut, almond flour and stevia into a food processor and blend until smooth.
2. Melt the coconut oil in the microwave and combine it with the vanilla and ground pistachio nuts in a mixing bowl, mashing with a fork.
3. Combine the almond flour mixture with the coconut oil and pistachio mixture in a mixing bowl.
4. Whisk the eggs and add them into the sweet almond-coconut oil mixture.
5. Form 12 fat bombs out of the mixture and bake them at 330°- 350° Fahrenheit for 15 minutes, then cool and serve.

Nutrients per serving:

Total Carbs: 9g

Net Carbs: 6g

Total Fat: 17g

Protein: 9g

Calories: 159

20. Choco Almonds-Coconut Butter Fat Bombs

***Preparation time:** 20 minutes*

***Cooking time:** 0 minutes*

***Servings:** 10*

Ingredients:
- 4 oz coconut butter
- 4 oz almond butter
- 4 oz coconut oil
- 4 oz cocoa powder
- 15 drops of stevia
- cinnamon
- spray cream

Instructions:

1. Melt the coconut oil, coconut butter and almond butter in the microwave and mix together.
2. Combine the cocoa powder, stevia and cinnamon with the coconut oil mixture in a mixing bowl, mashing with a fork until smooth.
3. Pour the mixture into the small silicone molds and place in the fridge for around 2 hours serving with the spray cream on top.

Nutrients per serving:

Total Carbs: 7g

Net Carbs: 4.1g

Total Fat: 19g

Protein: 8g

Calories: 187

21.Sweet Pine Nuts Fat Bombs

Preparation time: *25 minutes*

Cooking time: *0 minutes*

Servings: *12*

Ingredients:

- 4 oz ground pine nuts
- 2 oz shredded coconut
- 15 oz cottage cheese
- 4 oz unsalted butter
- 2 tablespoons coconut oil
- 2 oz cream
- 2 oz dark chocolate

- 10 drops of stevia
- vanilla
- cardamom

Instructions:

1. Melt the butter and the cottage cheese in a skillet.
2. Combine the coconut oil, shredded coconut, vanilla, cardamom, stevia, except for the chocolate and ground pine nuts. Add the mixture to the melted butter and cottage cheese and cool.
3. Melt the chocolate on a low heat, stirring and adding cream for around 10 minutes.
4. Form the fat bombs out of the mixture, slowly pour the melted chocolate over the fat bombs and sprinkle the grated pine nuts on top.
5. Sweet pine nuts fat bombs should be placed in the fridge for around 3 hours.

Nutrients per serving:

Total Carbs: 5g

Net Carbs: 4.1g

Total Fat: 18g

Protein: 7g

Calories: 134

22.Fresh Raspberries Fat Bombs

Preparation time: 20 minutes

Cooking time: 0 minutes

Servings: 15

Ingredients:

- 2 oz fresh raspberries
- 4 oz raspberry syrup
- 8 oz creamed coconut milk
- 4 oz unsalted butter
- 4 oz coconut oil
- 2 oz cocoa powder
- 15 drops of stevia
- spray cream

Instructions:

1. Combine the creamed coconut milk, unsalted butter and cocoa powder with coconut oil in a mixing bowl, mashing with a fork until smooth.
2. Pulse the stevia and raspberry syrup using a blender and mix them with coconut oil and unsalted butter mixture.
3. Pour the mixture into the ice cream maker and process for 1 hour.
4. Spoon the sweet mixture into the small silicone molds or an ice tray and freeze for around 4 hours, serving with a spray cream and raspberries on top.

Nutrients per serving:

Total Carbs: 7g

Net Carbs: 4.1g

Total Fat: 19g

Protein: 8g

Calories: 187

23.Peanuts Fat Bombs

Preparation time: 20 minutes

Cooking time: 0 minutes

Servings: 18

Ingredients:

- 8 oz peanut butter
- 8 oz coconut oil
- 4 oz cocoa powder
- 4 oz coconut flour
- 15 drops of stevia
- chocolate spray cream

Instructions:

1. Melt the unsalted butter and coconut oil in a skillet over medium heat.
2. Add all the remaining ingredients and melt on a low heat, stirring for around 15 minutes until they have a creamy and smooth consistency.
3. Cool and pour the mixture into each small silicone mold and freeze for 4 hours serving with a chocolate spray cream on top.

Nutrients per serving:

Total Carbs: 5.5g

Net Carbs: 3.9g

Total Fat: 15g

Protein: 6.2g

Calories: 154

24. Milk Chocolate and Strawberries Fat Bombs

Preparation time: 20 minutes

Cooking time: 0 minutes

Servings: 12

Ingredients:

- 9 oz strawberries
- 6 oz milk chocolate
- 3 oz cream cheese
- 5 oz unsalted butter
- 3 oz coconut oil
- 15 drops of stevia
- 2 tablespoons cocoa powder
- vanilla

Instructions:

1. Melt 6 oz of the milk chocolate in the microwave and pulse the strawberries using a blender.
2. Blend the cream cheese, butter, coconut oil, cocoa powder, stevia, chocolate, and vanilla until smooth using a food processor.
3. Combine the mixture with the pulsed strawberries in a mixing bowl, mashing with a fork, then place in the fridge for 2 hours.
4. Form 12 strawberry fat bombs out of the mixture and serve.

Nutrients per serving:

Total Carbs: 9g

Net Carbs: 6g

Total Fat: 14g

Protein: 7g

Calories: 95

25.Nuts Fat Bombs

Preparation time: 30 minutes

Cooking time: 0 minutes

Servings: 12

Ingredients:
- 8 oz macadamia nuts
- 4 oz almonds
- 2 teaspoons vanilla
- 5 oz unsalted butter
- 2 oz cream cheese
- 3 oz coconut oil
- 15 drops of stevia
- 3 tablespoons monk fruit sweetener

- walnuts
- spray cream

Instructions:

1. Grind the macadamia nuts and almonds and mix with the blended cream cheese and butter using a food processor.
2. Combine the mixture with the other ingredients except for the spray cream, mashing with a fork until smooth, and then place in the fridge for 2 hours.
3. Form 12 nuts fat bombs out of the mixture and add the walnut halves or the spray cream on top.

Nutrients per serving:

Total Carbs: 7.5g

Net Carbs: 4.8g

Total Fat: 13g

Protein: 7g

Calories: 65

26. Lemon Taste Fat Bombs

***Preparation time:* 20 minutes**

***Cooking time:* 0 minutes**

***Servings:* 15**

Ingredients:

- 3 tablespoons lemon zest, minced
- 7 oz dark chocolate
- 2 oz milk chocolate
- 8 oz coconut butter
- 3 oz coconut oil
- 3 oz cocoa powder
- 15 drops of stevia
- cinnamon

Instructions:

1. Melt the chocolate in your microwave and combine it with the stevia, cinnamon, coconut oil, coconut butter, lemon zest, and cocoa powder.
2. Spoon the mixture into each small paper muffin cup, candy cup or silicone candy mold and place in the fridge for around 3 hours.

Nutrients per serving:

Total Carbs: 4.1g

Net Carbs: 2.2g

Total Fat: 9g

Protein: 6g

Calories: 68

27. Raspberries Fat Bombs

Preparation time: 15 minutes

Cooking time: 0 minutes

Servings: 15

Ingredients:

- fresh raspberries
- 5 oz dark chocolate
- 8 oz cocoa butter
- 3 oz coconut oil
- 20 drops of stevia
- vanilla

- chocolate spray cream

Instructions:

1. Melt 5 oz of the dark chocolate in your microwave.
2. Melt the coconut oil and cocoa butter in a pan over low heat for 15 minutes.
3. Add the vanilla and stevia drops and mix all the ingredients except for the raspberries using a hand mixer.
4. Fill the paper muffin cups or candy cups with mixture and add the chocolate spray cream, raspberries on top and place in the fridge for around 3 hours.

Nutrients per serving:

Total Carbs: 4.4g

Net Carbs: 3.2g

Total Fat: 12g

Protein: 6g

Calories: 78

28. Dark Chocolate Fat Bombs

Preparation time: 20 minutes

Cooking time: 25 minutes

Servings: 10

Ingredients:

- 15 oz cottage cheese or curd
- 4 oz cream cheese
- 10 oz coconut butter
- 5 oz coconut oil
- 4 oz dark chocolate
- 5 oz cocoa powder
- 15 drops of stevia

Instructions:

1. Melt the coconut oil and coconut butter in a pan over low heat for 15 minutes.
2. Place the cottage cheese, cream cheese, stevia, cocoa powder, coconut oil, and coconut butter into a food processor and blend until they have a smooth and creamy consistency.
3. Form 10 fat bombs out of the mixture and place them in the fridge for 1 hour.
4. Melt the chocolate on a low heat, stirring for around 10 minutes.
5. Cool the mixture and slowly pour it over the fat bombs.
6. The fat bombs should be placed in the fridge for at least 2 hours.

Nutrients per serving:

Total Carbs: 8.9g

Net Carbs: 7g

Total Fat: 25g

Protein: 13g

Calories: 95

29. Blueberries Choco Fat Bombs

Preparation time: 25 minutes

Cooking time: 0 minutes

Servings: 12

Ingredients:

- 4 oz fresh blueberries
- 18 oz cottage cheese or curd
- 10 oz coconut butter
- 7 oz coconut oil
- 4 tablespoons monk fruit sweetener
- 15 drops of stevia
- 5 oz dark chocolate
- vanilla

Instructions:

1. Place the cottage cheese, stevia, coconut oil, and coconut butter into a food processor and blend until smooth.
2. Pulse the blueberries using a blender and mix them with the cottage cheese, stevia, coconut oil and coconut butter up to a homogeneous mass.
3. Form 12 fat bombs out of the mixture and place them in the fridge for 1 hour.
4. Melt the chocolate on low heat, stirring for around 10 minutes.
5. Cool the mixture and slowly pour it over the blueberries fat bombs.
6. Sprinkle cinnamon on top and place the fat bombs in the fridge for at least 5 hours.

Nutrients per serving:

Total Carbs: 9g

Net Carbs: 7.4g

Total Fat: 18g

Protein: 12g

Calories: 123

30. Wild Dried Berries Fat Bombs

Preparation time: 20 minutes

Cooking time: 10 minutes

Servings: 10

Ingredients:

- 5 oz dried blackcurrants
- 5 oz dried wild blueberries
- 5 oz dried strawberries
- 10 oz coconut butter
- 8 oz coconut oil
- 10 drops of stevia
- 4 tablespoons monk fruit sweetener
- 3 oz white chocolate

- 2 oz cream
- vanilla

Instructions:

1. Place all the ingredients except for the the white chocolate and cream into a food processor and blend until they have a smooth and creamy consistency.
2. Form 10 fat bombs out of the mixture and place them in the fridge for 50 minutes.
3. Melt the chocolate on low heat, stirring and adding cream for around 10 minutes.
4. Cool the mixture and slowly pour it over the fat bombs.
5. Freeze the fat bombs for at least 2 hours and then you are free to serve them.

Nutrients per serving:

Total Carbs: 9g

Net Carbs: 7.8g

Total Fat: 18g

Protein: 9.5g

Calories: 157

Conclusion

Thank you for having patience and trying the sweet keto fat bomb recipes from this cookbook.

If you are new in the field of sweet keto fat bombs, this cookbook will help you to start your sweet keto journey. Hope that you enjoy and have as much fun preparing and experimenting with sweet fat bomb recipes as I had while creating these sweet bomb desserts for You!

Part 2

Introduction

The ketogenic (keto) diet is the most powerful and effective diet available on the market today. This Keto Fat Bomb recipe book is for every keto beginner. In this book, you will find quick and easy recipes for sweet and savory snacks that will give you the energy boost you need from morning till evening. These amazing sweet and savory recipes will help your body reach ketosis in the most delicious way so you can burn fat, feel amazing and look your best.

These keto fat bombs give you instant energy and save you from consuming foods with excess carbohydrates (carbs) especially during special holidays and occasions. In this book, you are going to find a wonderful collection of great tasting fat bombs that are going to have you feasting across the seasons. The keto fat bombs are the perfect low carb, high-fat treats that are so good you will not even feel like you are on a diet. With these easy recipes, you'll always have something delicious and satisfying to snack on while following the ketogenic diet.

You can have these fat bombs as a breakfast, snack, dessert, or meal replacement. You can eat these sweet and savory snacks during different times of the day. Regardless of how you choose to consume these keto fat bombs, you are sure to get a significant boost of energy every time you put one into your mouth.

Chapter 1: The Ketogenic Diet

What is the Keto diet?

The ketogenic diet is a diet that is high in fat, low in carbs and moderate in protein. Usually, the macronutrient ratio in terms of calories sits within the following ranges:

- 5 to 10% of calories from carbs
- 15 to 30% of calories from protein
- 60 to 75% or more of calories from fat

You need to limit your total carb intake to follow the ketogenic diet. As the ketogenic diet is a high-fat diet, most of your daily energy intake should come from fats. Increasing your fat intake and lowering your carbohydrate intake leads to a beneficial metabolic state known as ketosis.

-

What is Ketosis?

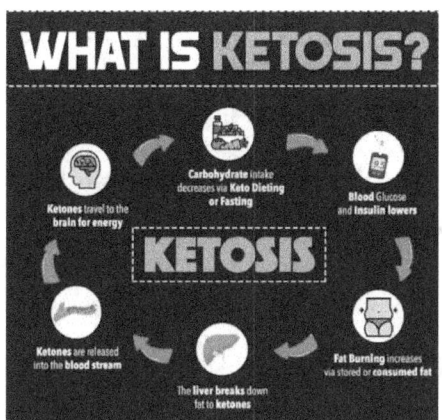

After carbs, the body's second preferred source of energy is fat. When carbohydrates are not easily available, your body turns to fat to get vital energy. The liver will break down the fat into fatty acids, which then break down into an energy-rich substance called ketones. When your body starts to burn fat instead of carbohydrates for energy, the process is called ketosis. The aim of the ketogenic diet is to transform your body into a fat burning machine by entering into long-term ketosis.

When increasing your fat intake, always opt for healthy fats:

- Saturated fats (tallow, lard, chicken fat, duck fat, goose fat, clarified butter/ghee, butter, coconut oil).
- Monounsaturated fats (olive oil, macadamia oil, and avocado oil)

- Polyunsaturated fatty acids, especially omega-3s from fatty fish and seafood. Both omega-3 and omega-6 fatty acids are essential. The aim is to balance your omega-3 and omega-6 ration.

Avoid unhealthy fats such as vegetable oils (canola, cottonseed safflower, sunflower, soybean, corn oil, etc.), and trans fats such as margarine.

Benefits of the ketogenic diet:

- Weight loss: The fat-rich ketogenic diet promotes considerable weight loss. Your insulin levels drop when you are on a ketogenic diet, which turns your body into a fat burning machine.
- Control blood sugar: The ketogenic diet lower blood sugar levels. Studies show that the ketogenic diet is a more effective way to prevent diabetes than low-calorie diets.
- Mental focus: The ketogenic diet can help enhance mental performance of dieters. This is because ketones are a great source of fuel for the brain. By preventing big blood sugar spikes, you trigger a positive effect on your focus and concentration.
- Increased energy and normalized hunger: Fat has been shown to be the most effective fuel to burn as an energy source. Fat rich foods make you more energetic during the day. Additionally, fat is more satisfying, so you feel full longer.

A complete keto food guide

Protein

Liberally:
- Fatty fish like salmon
- Grass-fed beef
- Dark meat, chicken

Occasionally:
- Bacon
- Low-fat proteins, like skinless chicken breast, and shrimp

Never:
- Cold cuts with added sugar
- Meat that has been marinated in sugary sauces
- Fish or chicken nuggets

Oil and Fats

Liberally:
- Butter
- Heavy cream
- Avocado oil
- Coconut oil
- Olive oil

Occasionally:
- Safflower oil
- Sunflower oil
- Corn oil

Never:
- Artificial trans fats
- Margarine

Fruits and Veggies

Liberally:
- Celery
- Asparagus
- Avocado
- Leafy greens, such as arugula and spinach

Occasionally:
- Leeks
- Eggplant
- Spaghetti squash

Never:
- Corn
- Potatoes
- Raisins

Nuts and Seeds

Liberally:
- Walnuts

- Almonds
- Flax and chia seeds

Occasionally:

- Cashews
- Pistachios
- Unsweetened nut butter

Never:

- Trail mixes with dried fruit
- Sweetened nut or seed butter
- Chocolate-covered nuts

Dairy Products

Liberally:

- Cheddar cheese
- Feta cheese
- Blue cheese

Occasionally:

- Full-fat cottage cheese
- Full-fat ricotta cheese
- Full-fat plain Greek yogurt

Never:

- Milk
- Ice cream
- Sweetened nonfat yogurt

Sweeteners

<u>**Liberally:**</u> Practice moderation with sweeteners

Occasionally:

- Stevia
- Xylitol
- Erythritol

Never:

- Maple syrup
- Agave
- White and brown sugars
- Honey

Condiments and Sauces

Liberally:

- Guacamole
- Mayonnaise
- Lemon butter sauce

Occasionally:

- Raw garlic
- Tomato sauce (no added sugar)
- Balsamic vinegar

Never:

- Ketchup

- Honey mustard
- Barbecue sauce

Drinks

Liberally:

- Bone Broth
- Plain tea
- Almond milk
- Water

Occasionally:

- Unsweetened carbonated water
- Black coffee
- Zero-calorie drinks

Never:

- Fruit juice
- Soda
- Lemonade

Herbs and Spices

Liberally: All herbs and spices fit in a keto diet

- Cayenne, thyme, oregano, and paprika
- Pepper
- Salt

Occasionally:
- Ground ginger
- Garlic powder
- Onion powder

Never:
- Spice mixed with added sugar and artificial ingredients

Basic principles of the Keto diet:
- Ideally, the macronutrient ratio should be 60 to 75% of calories from fat, 15 to 30% calories from protein and 5 to 10% calories from carbohydrates.
- To get into ketosis, your daily carb intake should be less than 50 grams, ideally 20 to 30 grams. Most people stay in ketosis with around 20 to 30 grams of carbs daily.
- The daily proportion of calories that come from healthy fats should be increased.
- Protein consumption should be moderate.
- Sodium, potassium, and magnesium may become deficient during ketosis. Drink bone broth daily, and add more salt to your meals. Eat more potassium-rich foods and take a magnesium supplement.
- Eat only when you feel hungry.
- Stop eating when you feel full.
- Stay hydrated.

- When starting the keto diet, start using macronutrient counting apps or specific keto apps.

Chapter 2: Fat Bombs

Fat bombs

Fat bombs are low-carb, high-fat recipes or foods that include a high percentage of fat and a low percentage of carbohydrates. Fat bombs were originally created as pure fat snacks to reach your fat macronutrient goal for the day when following a ketogenic diet. Over time, and with the widespread use of the diet, the concept of the fat bomb has widened a little to include small meals with an adequate ratio of protein to fat that also keep the carbohydrate content to a minimum. If you are on a low-carb diet, ensuring that your diet contains enough healthy fats can be tricky, especially if you are new to a keto diet.

While most fat bombs should be used as occasional treats, not meal replacements, there is an exception to the rule. Here is how to include fat bombs in your diet:

- Use them to boost your fat intake to meet your macronutrient targets.
- Enjoy a fat bomb when you don't have time to cook and need a quick hit of energy.
- Use them as pre- or post-workout snacks.
- Try fat bombs if you are on a fat fast

A few facts about ketogenic fat bombs:

1. Ketogenic fat bombs are often small. It is hard to eat too many of them, so they take the shape of small balls or mini muffins.
2. Fat bombs can be sweet or savory. Most fat bombs are usually sweetened by keto approved sweeteners such as stevia.
3. Fat bombs contain lots of healthy fats. Most ketogenic fat bombs contain coconut butter or coconut oil as an ingredient.
4. Store your fat bombs in the refrigerator: Fat bombs are made from lots of fat, which is often liquid at room temperature. Make sure to keep them in the fridge when you are not eating them. They will usually last 1 to 2 weeks in the refrigerator in an airtight container. You can also freeze them.
5. Fat bombs often also contain seeds and nuts.

Essential fat bomb ingredients:

- Nuts
- Seeds
- Coconut
- Coconut oil
- Cocoa butter
- Full-fat dairy

There are 3 basic ingredients in every fat bomb recipe.

1. Healthy fats:
- Cocoa butter
- Coconut butter
- Almond butter
- Coconut oil
- Coconut milk
- Coconut cream
- Butter
- Bacon fat
- Avocado oil

2. Flavoring:
- Sugar-free vanilla extract
- 100% dark chocolate
- Cocoa powder
- Salt
- Peppermint extract
- Spices

3. Texture
- Cacao Nibs
- Almonds
- Pecans
- Walnuts
- Chia seeds
- Bacon Bits
- Shredded coconut

Activated nuts and seeds:

Activated (soaking or sprouting) nuts and seeds are best because they are more easily digested, and nutrients are better absorbed. Soaking nuts is far more effective than roasting. Also, soaking and drying them produces a crunchier texture and more delicious flavor.

Soaking guidelines:

- Almonds: Soak for 8 to 12 hours
- Hazelnuts: Soak for 8 to 12 hours
- Pine nuts: Soak for 4 to 8 hours
- Walnuts: Soak for 4 to 8 hours
- Pecans: Soak for 4 to 8 hours
- Brazil nuts: Soak for 4 to 8 hours
- Macadamia nuts: Soak for 4 to 8 hours
- Cashews: Soak for 2 to 3 hours
- Pistachios: Soak for 2 to 3 hours

Coconut products:

- Desiccated coconut. It is shredded and dehydrated coconut meat.
- Coconut butter. It is made from dehydrated coconut meat.
- Coconut flour. It is finely ground flour made from coconut meat.

- Coconut milk. It is the liquid extracted from the grated meat of the coconut.
- Coconut cream. It is the fatty part of coconut milk that has been separated from the watery part.
- Coconut oil. It is fat extracted from the meat of mature coconuts.

Cocoa and Chocolate

- Cacao butter or cocoa butter. It is pure fat extracted from cacao beans.
- Cocoa Paste. It is pure cacao mass and becomes liquid when heated.
- Cocoa powder. Raw cocoa powder is made from raw cacao mass.
- Cacao Nibs. They are cacao beans that have been roasted, separated from their husks, and crushed into smaller pieces.
- Dark chocolate. It is made with a minimum of 70% cacao solids.

The main steps in cooking fat bombs:

Step 1: combine all the needed ingredients in a mixing bowl, in a blender or in a food processor. If using solid fat, melt it slightly in the microwave.

Step 2: Pour the mixture into muffin cups or into a baking pan, or just use your hands to form the needed shape.

Step 3: Refrigerate or freeze for several hours for the texture to become solid. Cut into pieces if you are using a baking pan.

Special instructions for making fat bombs:

- Dividing coconut milk for coconut cream: Buy a 13.4 ounce can of full-fat organic coconut milk and put it in the refrigerator overnight. In the morning, flip the can upside down and open it. Pour out the coconut water, and then scoop out the cream, which will be solid.
- Cooking prosciutto and making prosciutto crumbles: Preheat the oven to 350°F. Place thin prosciutto slices on a cookie sheet and bake for 12 minutes. Remove from the oven and let cool. Once cold and crispy, chop finely with a sharp kitchen knife until reduced to crumbles.

Chapter 3: Sweet Fat Bomb Recipes

Keto Chocolate Coconut Candies

Prep time: **1 hour 15 minutes**/Cooking time: **0 minute**/Servings: **9**

Ingredients
- Coconut oil – 1 cup
- Cocoa powder – 1 cup
- Powdered erythritol – ¼ cup
- Vanilla bean powder – 1 tsp.
- Stevia extract – 15 drops
- Salt to taste

- Coconut butter – ¼ cup, chilled

Method

1. Melt coconut oil in a microwave. Combine with the next four ingredients.
2. Spoon about ½ of the chocolate mixture into silicone molds. Refrigerate for 15 minutes.
3. Remove from the refrigerator and add ½ teaspoon coconut butter into each mold.
4. Top with the remaining chocolate mixture and refrigerate for 40 minutes.
5. Serve.

Nutritional Facts Per Serving
- Calories: 76
- Fat: 7.7 g
- Carb: 1 g
- Protein: 1 g

Neapolitan Fat Bombs

Prep time: 2 hours 50 minutes/**Cooking time:** 0 minute/ **Servings:** 24

Ingredients
- Butter – ½ cup
- Coconut oil – ½ cup
- Sour cream – ½ cup
- Cream cheese – ½ cup
- Erythritol – 2 Tbsp.
- Liquid stevia – 25 drops
- Cocoa powder – 2 Tbsp.
- Vanilla extract – 1 tsp.
- Strawberries – 2, puréed

Method
1. Blend the first six ingredients in a bowl.

2. Divide the mixture into 3 different bowls. Stir cocoa powder into the first bowl, strawberries into the second, and vanilla into the third.
3. Pour cocoa powder mixture into fat bomb molds.
4. Put in the freezer for 30 minutes. Repeat with the vanilla mixture forming a second layer.
5. Freeze vanilla mixture for 30 minutes.
6. Finally repeat with the strawberry mixture.
7. Freeze all again for at least 1 hour.
8. Serve.

Nutritional Facts Per Serving
- Calories: 102
- Fat: 11 g
- Carb: 1 g
- Protein: 1 g

Keto Coconut Fat Bombs

Prep time: **50 minutes**/Cooking time: **5 minute**/Servings: **12**

Ingredients
- Shredded coconut – 1½ cups, unsweetened
- Extra-virgin coconut oil – ¼ cup
- Butter – ¼ cup
- Cinnamon – ¼ tsp.
- Salt to taste

Method

1. Preheat the oven to 375°F.
2. Toast the coconut on a baking tray for 5 minutes, and then pulse it in a blender.

3. Add the remaining ingredients and stir to mix.
4. Fill 12 mini-muffin forms with 1½ tablespoons of the mixture.
5. Refrigerate for 30 minutes.
6. Serve.

Nutritional Facts Per Serving
- Calories: 104
- Fat: 9.6 g
- Carb: 1 g
- Protein: 1.9 g

Lemon Fat Bombs

Prep time: 1 hour 15 minutes/**Cooking time:** 0 minute/**Servings:** 16

Ingredients

- Coconut butter – 7 oz. softened
- Extra-virgin coconut oil – ¼ cup, softened
- Organic lemon zest – 1 to 2 Tbsp. minced
- Stevia extract – 20 drops

Method

1. Mix all the ingredients in a bowl.
2. Pour 1 tablespoon of the coconut mixture into each small muffin paper cup and place on a tray.
3. Refrigerate for 1 hour and serve.

Nutritional Facts Per Serving

- Calories: 112
- Fat: 11.9 g
- Carb: 3 g
- Protein: 1 g

Vanilla Fat Bombs

Prep time: 50 minutes/**Cooking time:** 0 minute/**Servings:** 14

Ingredients

- Unsalted Macadamia nuts – 1 cup
- Extra-virgin coconut oil – ¼ cup
- Butter – ¼ cup
- Vanilla extract – 2 tsp.
- Stevia extract – 20 drops
- Powdered erythritol – 2 Tbsp.

Method

1. Pulse the macadamia nuts in a blender. Combine them with softened butter and coconut oil.
2. Add the remaining ingredients. Mix well.

3. Fill each of 12 mini-muffin cups with 1½ tablespoons of the mixture.
4. Refrigerate for 30 minutes.
5. Serve

Nutritional Facts Per Serving

- Calories: 132
- Fat: 14.4 g
- Carb: 4 g
- Protein: 2 g

Chocolate Peanut Butter Fat Bombs

Prep time: 30 minutes/**Cooking time:** 0 minute/**Servings**: 8

Ingredients
- Coconut oil – ½ cup
- Cocoa powder – ¼ cup
- Hemp seeds – 6 Tbsp., hulled
- Heavy cream – 2 Tbsp.
- Vanilla extract – 1 tsp.
- Liquid stevia – 28 drops
- Unsweetened coconut – ¼ cup, shredded

Method

1. Combine all the ingredients, except for the shredded coconut.

2. Mix to a creamy consistency.
3. Form balls out of the mixture.
4. Roll balls in the coconut.
5. Put them on a baking tray lined with parchment paper.
6. Freeze for 20 minutes and serve.

Nutritional Facts Per Serving
- Calories: 208
- Fat: 20 g
- Carb: 3 g
- Protein: 4.4 g

Red Velvet Fat Bombs

Prep time: 55 minutes/**Cooking time:** 0 minute/**Servings:** 24

Ingredients

- 90% dark chocolate – 3.5 oz.
- Cream cheese – 4.5 oz. softened
- Butter – 3.5 oz. softened
- Stevia – 1 tsp.
- Vanilla extract – 1 tsp.
- Red food coloring – 4 drops
- Heavy cream – ⅓ cup, whipped

Method

1. Melt chocolate in the microwave.
2. Combine the remaining ingredients, except for the whipped cream, with a hand mixer.

3. Add the melted chocolate and mix well.
4. Fill a piping bag with the mixture and transfer the fat bomb mixture onto a lined tray.
5. Refrigerate for 40 minutes.
6. Top with whipped cream.
7. Cut into servings and serve.

Nutritional Facts Per Serving

- Calories: 85
- Fat: 9 g
- Carb: 2 g
- Protein: 1 g

Almond Pistachio Fat Bombs

Prep time: 8 hours and 30 minutes/**Cooking time:** 0 minute/**Servings:** 36 squares

Ingredients
- Cocoa butter – ½ cup, melted
- All natural roasted almond butter – 1 cup
- Creamy coconut butter – 1 cup
- Coconut oil – 1 cup, firm
- Full-fat coconut milk – ½ cup
- Ghee – ¼ cup
- Pure vanilla extract – 1 Tbsp.
- Chai spice – 2 tsp.
- Pure almond extract – ¼ tsp.
- Salt – ¼ tsp.
- Raw shelled pistachios – ¼ cup, chopped

Method

1. Microwave the cocoa butter until melted.
2. Combine all the ingredients, except the pistachios and cocoa butter. Mix with a hand mixer.
3. Pour the melted cocoa butter into the almond butter mixture. Mix well.
4. Transfer the mixture to a baking pan; sprinkle with pistachios.
5. Refrigerate overnight.
6. Cut into 36 squares and serve.

Nutritional Facts Per Serving
- Calories: 170
- Fat: 17.4 g
- Carb: 3 g
- Protein: 2.2 g

Espresso Fat Bombs

*Prep time: **4 hours 20 minutes**/Cooking time: **0 minute**/Servings: **24***

Ingredients
- Unsalted butter – 5 Tbsp., softened
- Cream cheese – 3 oz., softened
- Espresso – 2 oz.
- Coconut oil – 4 Tbsp.
- Heavy whipping cream – 2 Tbsp.
- Monk fruit sweetener – 2 Tbsp.

Method

1. Melt together all the ingredients, except for the sweetener, in a double boiler for 3 to 4 minutes.

2. Add the sweetener. Mix all the ingredients with a hand mixer.
3. Spoon the mixture into silicon muffin molds.
4. Freeze for 4 hours.
5. Remove fat bombs from the silicon molds.
6. Serve.

Nutritional Facts Per Serving
- Calories: 63
- Fat: 6.8 g
- Carb: 1.3 g
- Protein: 1 g

Peanut Butter Chocolate Chip Fat Bombs

Prep time: 4 hours 10 minutes/**Cooking time:** 0 minute/**Servings:** 24

Ingredients
- Cream cheese – 8 oz.
- Peanut butter – 6 to 8 Tbsp.
- Butter – 2 Tbsp.
- Vanilla – 1 Tbsp.
- Xylitol sweetener – 1 to 2 Tbsp.
- Dark chocolate chips – 9 oz., no sugar added

Method
1. Mix all the ingredients, except for the chocolate chips, with a hand mixer.
2. Stir in the chocolate chips.
3. Place the mixture in silicone candy molds.

4. Freeze for 4 hours.
5. Serve.

Nutritional Facts Per Serving
- Calories: 63
- Fat: 6 g
- Carb: 3.5 g
- Protein: 1.5 g

Coconut & Almond Fat Bombs

Prep time: **1 hour 5 minutes**/Cook time: **5 minutes**/Servings: **15**

Ingredients
- Unsalted butter – 1.7 oz.
- Ricotta cheese 14 oz.
- Liquid stevia – 20 drops
- Psyllium husks – 1 Tbsp.
- Coconut – ⅓ cup, shredded
- Cardamom – ¾ tsp.
- Vanilla extract – ½ tsp.
- Coconut oil – 2 Tbsp.
- Almonds – ⅔ cup

Method

1. In a saucepan, melt the butter and mix in the ricotta.
2. Combine all the ingredients, except for the shredded coconut and almonds. Add the mixture to the melted cheese mixture. Cool.
3. Roll the mixture into balls, and press an almond inside of each.
4. Roll the balls in shredded coconut to coat.
5. Refrigerate for 30 minutes.
6. Serve.

Nutritional Facts Per Serving
- Calories: 136
- Fat: 13 g
- Carb: 2 g
- Protein: 3 g

Pumpkin Spice Fat Bombs

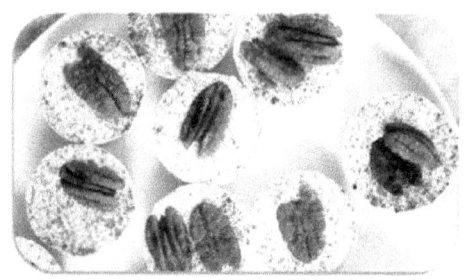

*Prep time: **4 hours 10 minutes**/Cooking time: **10 minutes**/Servings: **24***

Ingredients
- Pecans – ½ cup
- Coconut oil – ½ cup
- Cream cheese – 4 oz., softened
- Pumpkin purée – ½ cup
- Monk fruit sweetener – ¼ cup
- Pumpkin pie spice – 2 tsp.
- Cinnamon – ¼ tsp.

Method

1. Toast pecans until fragrant.
2. Melt coconut oil and cream cheese until combined.
3. Mix all ingredients in a bowl.

4. Spoon the mixture into silicone molds.
5. Top with toasted pecans and sprinkle with cinnamon.
6. Freeze for 4 hours.
7. Serve.

Nutritional Facts Per Serving
- Calories: 78
- Fat: 8.2 g
- Carb: 3.1 g
- Protein: 1 g

Berries and Cream Fat Bombs

Prep time: **8 hours 5 minutes**/Cooking time: **0 minute**/Servings: **24**

Ingredients
- Mixed berries – 2 cups, frozen
- Butter – 6 Tbsp., softened
- Cream cheese – 8 oz., softened
- Golden monk fruit sweetener – 2 Tbsp.
- Vanilla extract – 1 tsp.

Method

1. Microwave frozen berries until thawed, about 1 minute.

2. Blend all ingredients in a food processor.
3. Spoon mixture into silicon molds and freeze for overnight.
4. Pop fat bombs out of the molds and serve.

Nutritional Facts Per Serving
- Calories: 61
- Fat: 6 g
- Carb: 2.9 g
- Protein: 1 g

Raspberry, Chocolate, and Coconut Bark

Prep time: 1 hour 10 minutes/**Cooking time:** 8 minutes/**Servings:** 16

Ingredients

- Flaked coconut – ⅓ cup, unsweetened
- Macadamia nuts – ½ cup
- Coconut butter – 1 cup
- Coconut oil – ¼ cup
- Cocoa powder – ⅓ cup, unsweetened
- Powdered erythritol – ¼ cup
- Raspberries – ½ cup
- Sea salt to taste

Method

1. Preheat the oven to 350°F.

2. Toast the coconut flakes and macadamia nuts on a baking sheet 8 minutes until golden.
3. Melt the coconut butter and coconut oil in a double boiler. Mix in the cocoa powder and erythritol.
4. Pour the coconut-chocolate mixture onto a medium-size plate. Scatter the raspberries, toasted macadamia nuts and coconut over the chocolate.
5. Sprinkle with the sea salt.
6. Refrigerate for 1 hour.
7. Break the bark into pieces and serve.

Nutritional Facts Per Serving

- Calories: 248
- Fat: 25.4 g
- Carb: 7.6 g
- Protein: 2.4 g

Keto Macaroon Fat Bombs

Prep time: 15 minutes/**Cooking time:** 15 minutes/**Servings:** 10

Ingredients
- Almond flour – ¼ cup
- Coconut – ½ cup, shredded
- Swerve – 2 Tbsp.
- Vanilla extract – 1 Tbsp.
- Coconut oil – 1 Tbsp.
- Egg whites – 3, whisked

Method
1. Blend the first three ingredients.
2. In a small saucepan, melt the coconut oil and mix in the vanilla extract.
3. Mix together the melted coconut oil and almond flour mixture.

4. Whisk the egg whites. Fold them into the flour mix.
5. Form the mixture into balls.
6. Place the balls onto a cookie sheet.
7. Bake at 350°F for 8 minutes.
8. Remove from the oven, cool and serve.

Nutritional Facts Per Serving
- Calories: 46
- Fat: 5 g
- Carb: 1 g
- Protein: 2 g

Keto Chocolate Fat Bombs

Prep time: 10 minutes/**Cooking time:** 0 minute/**Servings:** 12

Ingredients
- Cocoa powder – 1 Tbsp.
- Chocolate protein powder – 2 Tbsp.
- Coconut milk – 4 Tbsp.
- Coconut flour – 2 Tbsp.
- Coconut – 2 Tbsp., shredded
- Cacao nibs – 1 Tbsp.
- Coconut oil – 1 tsp., softened
- Coconut butter – ⅔ cup, softened

Method
1. Combine all ingredients, except coconut oil and coconut butter, in a bowl. Whisk to mix well.

2. Spoon mixture into silicon molds.
3. Refrigerate for 30 minutes.
4. Mix coconut oil with coconut butter in a bowl. Remove molds from the refrigerator, and cover with coconut oil and butter coating.
5. Place back in the refrigerator until coating has hardened, about 1 hour.

Nutritional Facts Per Serving
- Calories: 138
- Fat: 14.47 g
- Carb: 2.55 g
- Protein: 1 g

Chocolate Peanut Butter Balls

Prep time: 10 minutes /**Cooking tim**e: 0 minute/**Servings:** 12

Ingredients
- Butter – ½ stick (2 oz.), softened
- Natural peanut butter – ½ cup
- Vanilla whey protein powder – 2 Tbsp.
- Sugar-free chocolate bars – ½ cup, melted
- Vanilla extract – 1 tsp.
- Powdered xylitol sweetener – 1½ cup

Method
1. Mix butter and peanut butter in a bowl with a hand mixer until smooth.
2. Add vanilla extract and protein powder, mix well.
3. Add sweetener and mix well.
4. Roll the dough into 24 bite-size balls.

5. Place balls on a pan lined with parchment paper.
6. Coat each ball with melted chocolate.
7. Refrigerate for 2 hours.
8. Serve.

Nutritional Facts Per Serving
- Calories: 126
- Fat: 12 g
- Carb: 2.54 g
- Protein: 3 g

Walnut Muffin Fat Bombs

Prep time: 20 minutes/**Cooking time:** 0 minute/**Servings:** 18

Ingredients
- Walnuts – 1½ cups, chopped
- Dark chocolate – 4.4 oz. (90% cocoa)
- Natural orange extract – 1 tsp.
- Fresh orange peel – 1 tsp.
- Extra-virgin coconut oil – 4 Tbsp.
- Liquid stevia – 15 to 20 drops
- Cinnamon – 1 tsp.

Method
1. Melt the chocolate in a double boiler.
2. Add cinnamon, oil, and stevia. Mix well.

3. Add fresh orange peel and natural orange extract. Add chopped walnuts and mix well.
4. Spoon mixture into small paper muffin cups.
5. Place in the fridge until solid, about 4 to 6 hours.

Nutritional Facts Per Serving
- Calories: 131
- Fat: 13 g
- Carb: 3 g
- Protein: 13 g

Cinnamon Fat Bombs

Prep time: 1 hour 30 minutes/**Cooking time**: 0 minute/**Servings:** 12

Ingredients
- Coconut milk – 1 cup
- Almond butter – 1 cup
- Vanilla extract – 1 tsp.
- Cinnamon – ¾ tsp.
- Nutmeg – ½ tsp.
- Natural sweetener – 1 tsp.
- Coconut – 1 cup, shredded

Method

1. Add all ingredients, except shredded coconut, to a double boiler. Stir constantly to melt and combine well.
2. When ready, remove from the heat and cool for 5 minutes.
3. Refrigerate for 45 minutes until hard.
4. Put the shredded coconut in a bowl.
5. Roll the cinnamon-coconut mixture into one-inch balls and roll them in the shredded coconut.
6. Place the balls on a serving plate and refrigerate for 2 to 3 hours.

Nutritional Facts Per Serving
- Calories: 184
- Fat: 20 g
- Carb: 1.6 g
- Protein: 1 g

Keto Orange Fat Bites

Prep time: **10 minutes/**Cooking time: **0 minute/**Servings: **14**

Ingredients
- Heavy whipping cream – ¼ cup
- Cream cheese – ½ cup
- Coconut oil – ½ cup, melted
- Pure orange extract – 1 tsp.
- Liquid stevia – 10 drops

Method
1. Blend all ingredients together.
2. Spoon the batter into paper muffin cups.
3. Refrigerate for 2 hours.
4. Remove from muffin cups and serve.

Nutritional Facts Per Serving
- Calories: 127
- Fat: 14 g
- Carb: 0.5 g
- Protein: 1 g

Blueberry Fat Bombs

Prep time: **15 minutes** /Cooking time: **0 minute**/Servings: **6**

Ingredients

- Butter – 5 Tbsp.
- Coconut oil – 3 Tbsp.
- Sugar-free blueberry syrup – 2 Tbsp.
- Cocoa powder – 2 Tbsp.

Method

1. Cook all ingredients in a saucepan over low heat until well combined.
2. Transfer into silicone molds and freeze for at least 3 hours.
3. Serve.

Nutritional Facts Per Serving

- Calories: 148
- Fat: 17 g
- Carb: 1 g
- Protein: 0.5 g

Cream Cheese Jello Balls

Prep time: 10 minutes /**Cooking time:** 0 minute/**Servings:** 8

Ingredients
- Cream cheese – 1 cup
- Coconut butter – ¼ cup
- Sugar-free jello powder – 1 package

Method
1. Put jello powder in a bowl.
2. In another bowl, combine coconut butter and cream cheese.
3. Take a teaspoon of the cream cheese mixture and roll into a ball in your hands, and then roll it in the jello powder. Make 16 balls

4. Cover with plastic wrap and refrigerate for 2 hours.

Nutritional Facts Per Serving
- Calories: 150
- Fat: 16 g
- Carb: 1 g
- Protein: 2 g

Almond Cookie Fat Bombs

Prep time: 25 minutes /**Cooking time:** 18 minutes/**Servings:** 16

Ingredients
- Almonds – 1 cup, chopped
- Butter – 1 cup, softened
- Almond flour – 2¼ cups
- Cocoa powder – 1¼ cup
- Coconut flour – 3½ tsp.
- Eggs – 2
- Stevia powder – ¾ cup
- Vanilla extract – 2 tsp.
- Baking soda – ½ tsp.
- Sea salt – ¼ tsp.

Method
1. Preheat the oven to 340°F.

2. Whisk the butter and sweetener together in a bowl.
3. Stir in the eggs and vanilla extract.
4. In another bowl mix together the almond flour, coconut flour, baking soda, cocoa powder, and salt.
5. Combine the egg mixture with the flour mixture.
6. Pour dough into a greased baking pan.
7. Sprinkle dough with chopped almonds.
8. Bake for 15 to 18 minutes.
9. Cool and cut into chunks.
10. Serve.

Nutritional Facts Per Serving
- Calories: 171
- Fat: 17 g
- Carb: 3.35 g
- Protein: 2.9 g

Lemon Coconut Fat Bombs

Prep time: 4 hours 15 minutes /**Cook time:** 0 minute/**Servings:** 12

Ingredients
- Shredded coconut – ¼ cup, unsweetened
- Cream cheese – 1 cup
- Pure lemon extract – 1 Tbsp.
- Natural sweetener of your choice to taste
- Butter – ¼ cup

Method
1. Combine cream cheese, butter, natural sweetener, and lemon extract in a bowl. Place bowl in the refrigerator for 15 to 20 minutes.
2. Add coconut to another bowl.
3. Roll lemon batter into 16 equal balls.

4. Dip each ball into coconut and place on a serving tray.
5. Refrigerate for 3 to 4 hours.
6. Serve.

Nutritional Facts Per Serving
- Calories: 106
- Fat: 12 g
- Carb: 1 g
- Protein: 1.3 g

Lemony Cream Cheese Bombshells

Prep time: 2 hours 10 minutes /**Cooking time:** 0 minute /**Servings:** 12

Ingredients
- Unsalted butter – ½ cup, softened
- Cream cheese – 1 cup, softened
- Pure lemon extract – ½ tsp.
- Granular stevia – ¾ cup

Method
1. Combine all ingredients with a hand mixer until soft.
2. Place teaspoonfuls of mixture on a wax paper-lined baking sheet.
3. Freeze until firm, at least 2 hours.
4. Remove from the freezer and serve.

Nutritional Facts Per Serving
- Calories: 134
- Fat: 14.5 g
- Carb: 1 g
- Protein: 1.3 g

Frozen Butter Rum Chocolate Fat Bombs

Prep time: 3 hours 15 minutes /**Cooking time:** 0 minute /**Servings:** 12

Ingredients
- Coconut oil – ¼ cup
- Almond butter – ¼ cup
- Rum extract – 2 tsp.
- Liquid stevia – 12 drops
- Cocoa powder – 2 Tbsp.

Method
1. Mix together all ingredients, except cocoa powder, in a saucepan over medium heat. Stir frequently until ingredients have melted. Turn off the heat.
2. Add cocoa powder and stir well to mix.
3. Pour mixture into 12 molds of a silicone-bottomed ice cube tray or silicone candy mold tray.

4. Freeze until set.
5. Serve.

Nutritional Facts Per Serving
- Calories: 75
- Fat: 7 g
- Carb: 2 g
- Protein: 2 g

Peppermint Fat Bombs

Prep time: 2 hours 10 minutes /**Cooking time:** 0 minute /**Servings:** 25

Ingredients
- Seed butter – 1¼ cup
- Peppermint extract – 1 tsp.
- Coconut oil – 1½ cups
- Natural sweetener – ½ cup
- Vanilla extract – 2 tsp.
- Salt – ¼ tsp.

Method
1. Melt the coconut oil in a pan over medium heat
2. Blend all ingredients with the oil until smooth.
3. When cool make 25 balls from the mixture.
4. Freeze the balls on a baking sheet until solid.
5. Serve.

Nutritional Facts Per Serving
- Calories: 202
- Fat: 19 g
- Carb: 3 g
- Protein: 22 g

Pistachio Fat Bombs

Prep time: **5 hours 15 minutes** /Cooking time: **0 minute** /Servings: **32**

Ingredients
- Almond butter – 1 cup, melted
- Ghee – ¼ cup
- Coconut oil – 1 cup
- Cocoa butter – ½ cup
- Pistachio nuts – ¼ cup
- Coconut milk – 1 Tbsp.
- Vanilla extract - 1 Tbsp.
- Masala chai – 2 tsp.

Method

1. Melt the cocoa butter over low heat in a saucepan.

2. In a bowl, combine all ingredients with a hand mixer, except pistachios, and cocoa butter.
3. Add in the melted butter and blend for 1 to 2 minutes more.
4. Transfer the mixture to a paper-lined, greased pan. Sprinkle with chopped pistachios and refrigerate for at least 5 hours.

Nutritional Facts Per Serving
- Calories: 147
- Fat: 17 g
- Carb: 1 g
- Protein: 1 g

Raspberry Fat Bombs

Prep time: 2 hours 20 minutes /**Cooking time:** 0 minute /**Servings:** 18

Ingredients
- Heavy cream – 3 Tbsp.
- Coconut oil – ¼ cup, melted
- Cream cheese – 8 oz. softened
- Raspberry extract – 3 tsp.
- Powdered erythritol – ½ cup
- Salt to taste
- Natural red food coloring – 5 drops

Method
1. Blend the cream cheese and sweetener together with a hand mixer.
2. Add the cream, food coloring, raspberry extract, and salt, and blend.

3. Add the coconut oil and continue to blend until it is smooth and creamy.
4. Refrigerate the mixture for 1 hour.
5. Then make 48 small balls from the batter and place on a parchment-lined baking sheet.
6. Place in the freezer for 2 hours.

Nutritional Facts Per Serving
- Calories: 101
- Fat: 1 2g
- Carb: 1 g
- Protein: 1 g

Mixed Berries Cheesecake Fat Bomb

Prep time: 2 hours 10 minutes /**Cooking time: 0** minute /**Servings:** 2

Ingredients
- Cream cheese – 4 oz., room temperature
- Butter – 4 Tbsp., room temperature
- Swerve natural sweetener – 2 tsp.
- Vanilla extract – 1 tsp.
- Mixed Berries – ¼ cup

Method
1. Blend the cream cheese, butter, sweetener, and vanilla with a hand mixer.
2. Mash the berries thoroughly in a bowl.
3. Add the mashed berries to the cream cheese mixture and mix well.

4. Spoon the cream cheese mixture into molds.
5. Freeze for at least 2 hours.

Nutritional Facts Per Serving
- Calories: 414
- Fat: 43 g
- Carb: 4 g
- Protein: 4 g

Pecan Fudge

Prep time: 45 minutes /**Cooking time:** 15 minutes/**Servings:** 60

Ingredients
- Butter – ½ cup (cubed) plus 1 tsp. for greasing
- Whipping cream – ½ cup
- Chopped pecans – 1 cup, toasted
- Vanilla extract – 1 tsp.
- Powdered sweetener – 1 cup

Method
1. Heat butter and cream in a saucepan. Bring to a boil, stirring constantly. cook until the soft ball stage.
2. Remove from the heat and add vanilla.
3. Let cool for 30 minutes.

4. Beat the fudge with a fork until it begins to thicken. Stir in the powdered sweetener gradually until smooth.
5. Add the nuts and stir.
6. Spread the fudge into a greased baking pan.
7. Cover with foil and cool in the fridge.
8. Remove the foil and cut into squares.

Nutritional Facts Per Serving
- Calories: 59
- Fat: 9 g
- Carb: 4 g
- Protein: 1 g

Chapter 4: Savory Fat Bombs

Smoked Mackerel Fat Bombs

Prep time: 10 minutes /**Cooking time:** 0 minute/**Servings:** 6

Ingredients
- Full-fat cream cheese – 3.5 oz., room temperature
- Unsalted butter – ¼ cup, room temperature
- Smoked mackerel fillets – 3.5 oz. (1 medium fillet)
- Lime juice – 1 Tbsp.
- Chopped fresh chives – 2 Tbsp.
- Cucumber slices for serving

Method
1. In a food processor, combine the lime juice, mackerel, butter, and cream cheese. Pulse until smooth. Transfer to a bowl.
2. Add the chives and mix with a spoon.
3. Refrigerate for 30 minutes or until set.
4. Enjoy as a dip with cucumber slices.

Nutritional Facts Per Serving
- Calories: 161
- Fat: 16.5 g
- Carb: 1 g
- Protein: 5 g

Bacon and Eggs Fat Bombs

Prep time: 40 minutes /**Cooking time:** 15 minutes/**Servings:** 6

Ingredients
- Eggs – 2, hard-boiled, cut into quarters
- Butter – ¼ cup
- Mayonnaise – 2 Tbsp.
- Bacon – 4 slices
- Salt and pepper to taste

Method
1. Preheat the oven to 375°F.
2. Cook the bacon slices on a baking tray for 15 minutes. Reserve the grease.
3. Cut the butter into pieces and add to the quartered eggs. Mash with a fork to mix.

4. Add the remaining ingredients, except for the bacon, and mix. Pour in the bacon grease and mix well. Refrigerate for 30 minutes.
5. Crumble the bacon.
6. Create 6 balls from the egg mixture and roll each ball in the crumbled bacon.
7. Serve.

Nutritional Facts Per Serving
- Calories: 185
- Fat: 18.4 g
- Carb: 0.2 g
- Protein: 5 g

Bacon and Guacamole Fat Bombs

Prep time: **40 minutes /**Cooking time: **15 minutes/**Servings: **6**

Ingredients

- Avocado – ½, peeled, and halved
- Butter – ¼ cup
- Garlic – 2 cloves, crushed
- Chili pepper – 1, chopped
- Cilantro – 2 Tbsp., chopped
- Lime juice – 1 Tbsp.
- Onion – ½, diced
- Bacon – 4 slices
- Salt and pepper to taste

Method

1. Preheat the oven to 375°F.

2. Cook the bacon strips on a baking tray for 15 minutes. Reserve the grease.
3. Combine the first six ingredients. Season with salt and pepper, and mix.
4. Add the onion and the bacon grease and mix. Refrigerate for 20 to 30 minutes.
5. Crumble the bacon. Create 6 balls from the mixture.
6. Roll each ball in the crumbled bacon.
7. Serve.

Nutritional Facts Per Serving

- Calories: 156
- Fat: 15.2 g
- Carb: 1.4 g
- Protein: 3.4 g

Pizza Fat Bombs

Prep time: 20 minutes **/Cooking time:** 0 minute/**Servings:** 6

Ingredients
- Cream cheese – 4 oz.
- Pepperoni – 14 slices
- Black olives – 8, pitted
- Sun-dried tomato pesto – 2 Tbsp.
- Chopped fresh basil – 2 Tbsp.
- Salt and pepper to taste

Method
1. Chop olives and pepperoni into small pieces.
2. Combine tomato pesto, basil, and cream cheese.
3. Mix the pepperoni and olives with the cream cheese mixture.
4. Form into balls. Serve.

Nutritional Facts Per Serving
- Calories: 101.3
- Fat: 9.62 g
- Carb: 1.69 g
- Protein: 2.3 g

Jalapeño Pepper Fat Bombs

Prep time: 20 minutes /**Cooking time:** 5 minutes/**Servings:** 6

Ingredients
- Cream cheese – 3 oz.
- Bacon – 3 slices
- Jalapeño pepper – 1, seeded
- Parsley – ½ tsp. dried
- Onion powder – ¼ tsp.
- Garlic powder – ¼ tsp.

- Salt and pepper to taste

Method

1. Fry bacon slices for 5 minutes, and then place them on paper towels. Save bacon grease.
2. Chop the jalapeño pepper. Mix together with spices, bacon fat, and cream cheese.
3. Make balls out of cream cheese mixture and roll them in the crumbled bacon.
4. Serve.

Nutritional Facts Per Serving
- Calories: 147
- Fat: 13.3 g
- Carb: 2.13 g
- Protein: 4.77 g

Bacon and Chicken Liver Fat Bombs

Prep time: **50 minutes** /Cooking time: **35 minutes/**Servings: **6**

Ingredients
- Bacon – 4 slices
- Unsalted butter – ⅓ cup, divided
- Chicken livers – 5.5 oz., diced
- Onion – ½, diced
- Garlic – 2 cloves, chopped
- Fresh sage – 1 Tbsp., chopped
- Salt and pepper to taste

Method

1. Preheat the oven to 325°F. Cook the bacon slices on a baking sheet for 30 minutes. Crumble the bacon and reserve the bacon grease.

2. Heat half of the butter in a skillet.
3. Add the livers and cook for 5 minutes. Pulse in a blender.
4. In another skillet, combine remaining butter, garlic, and onion. Cook for 10 minutes.
5. Transfer to the blender with the livers. Add the bacon grease and remaining ingredients, except for the bacon, and pulse. Refrigerate for 30 minutes.
6. Make 6 fat bombs from the mixture.
7. Roll them in the crumbled bacon.
8. Serve.

Nutritional Facts Per Serving
- Calories: 213
- Fat: 19.8g
- Carb: 1.2g
- Protein: 7g

Salmon and Dill Fat Bombs

Prep time: **35 minutes** /Cooking time: **0 minute**/Servings: 12

Ingredients
- Cream cheese – 1 cup
- Butter – ⅔ cup
- Smoked salmon – ½ package (2 oz.)
- Lemon juice to taste
- Dill to taste
- Salt to taste

Method
1. Place all ingredients in a food processor and blend.
2. Create small balls with the mixture and put them in the refrigerator for 30 minutes.
3. Serve cold.

Nutritional Facts Per Serving

- Calories: 174
- Fat: 13.4 g
- Carb: 0.3 g
- Protein: 3 g

Sesame Fat Bombs

Prep time: 30 minutes /**Cooking time**: 0 minute/**Servings:** 4

Ingredients
- Butter – 4 oz.
- Sesame oil – 2 Tbsp.
- Sea salt – 1 tsp.
- Red chili flakes – ¼ tsp.
- Sesame seeds – 2 tsp., toasted

Method
1. Toast the sesame seeds in a pan for 5 minutes. Set aside.
2. In a bowl, mix the remaining ingredients. Refrigerate for 15 minutes.
3. Make 4 fat bombs out of the mixture.

4. Roll each fat bomb in the toasted sesame seeds.
5. Serve.

Nutritional Facts Per Serving
- Calories: 123
- Fat: 4.5 g
- Carb: 0 g
- Protein: 2 g

Beef and Cheese Meatballs

Prep time: 10 minutes /**Cooking time**: 10 minutes/**Servings:** 9

Ingredients
- Beef – 1 lb. (16 oz.), ground
- Mozzarella cheese – 4 oz.
- Parmesan cheese – 3 Tbsp.
- Garlic powder – 1 tsp.
- Olive oil – 3 Tbsp.
- Salt and pepper to taste

Method
1. Cut the cheeses into cubes.
2. Combine the dry ingredients with the ground beef.
3. Roll the cubes of cheese with the beef, making 9 balls.

4. Fry the meatballs in olive oil for 10 minutes.
5. Chill and serve.

Nutritional Facts Per Serving
- Calories: 444
- Fat: 28 g
- Carb: 2 g
- Protein: 46 g

Cheesy Jalapeno Fat Bombs

Prep time: 1 hour and 20 minutes /**Cooking time:** 30 minutes /**Servings:** 6

Ingredients
- Full-fat cream cheese – 3.5 oz.
- Unsalted butter – ¼ cup
- Bacon slices – 4
- Cheddar cheese – ¼ cup, grated
- Jalapeño peppers – 2, seeded, chopped

Method
1. Preheat the oven to 325°F. Line a baking sheet with parchment paper.
2. Lay the bacon slices on the parchment.
3. Cook for 30 minutes in the oven.
4. Crumble the bacon in a bowl and reserve the grease.

5. Blend together the cream cheese and butter in a bowl.
6. Add the bacon grease, jalapeños, and cheddar cheese. Mix well. Refrigerate for 1 hour.
7. Make 6 fat bombs out of the mixture.
8. Roll them in the crumbled bacon.
9. Refrigerate for 1 hour.
10. Serve.

Nutritional Facts Per Serving
- Calories: 142
- Fat: 15 g
- Carb: 0.7 g
- Protein: 3.5 g

Avocado and Eggs Fat Bombs

Prep time: 1 hour and 20 minutes /**Cooking time:** 0 minute /**Servings:** 2

Ingredients
- Cooked egg yolks – 3
- Avocado – ½, peeled, pitted and chopped
- Mayonnaise – ¼ cup
- Lemon juice - 1 Tbsp.
- Spring onions – 2 Tbsp., chopped
- Salt and pepper to taste
- Cucumber slices and additional chopped spring onion for serving

Method
1. Blend chopped avocado and the remaining ingredients, except the egg yolks, in a food processor.
2. Mix the avocado mixture with the egg yolks.

3. Serve with cucumber slices and chopped spring onion.

Nutritional Facts Per Serving
- Calories: 147
- Fat: 14.8 g
- Carb: 1.1 g
- Protein: 2.2 g

Savory Salmon Fat Bombs

Prep time: **2 hours and 10 minutes** /Cooking time: **0 minute** /Servings: **6**

Ingredients
- Full-fat cream cheese – ½ cup
- Butter – ⅓ cup
- Smoked salmon – ½ package (2 oz.)
- Fresh lemon juice – 1 Tbsp.
- Dill – 1 to 2 Tbsp. chopped
- Lettuce leaves – 5

Method

1. Pulse all the ingredients, except the lettuce leaves, in a food processor.

2. Line a tray with parchment paper and make fat bombs using 2½ tablespoons of the mixture for each.
3. Refrigerate for 2 hours.
4. Garnish with more dill and place on top of lettuce leaves.
5. Serve.

Nutritional Facts Per Serving
- Calories: 147
- Fat: 15.7 g
- Carb: 0.7 g
- Protein: 3.2 g

Cheesy Pesto Fat Bombs

Prep time: 2 hours 5 minutes /**Cooking time:** 0 minute /**Servings:** 6

Ingredients
- Full-fat cream cheese – 1 cup
- Basil pesto – 2 Tbsp.
- Parmesan cheese – ½ cup, grated
- Green olives – 10, pitted and sliced
- Cucumber slices – 6

Method
1. Mix all the ingredients in a bowl.
2. Serve as a dip with sliced cucumbers or other fresh vegetables.
3. Also, you can refrigerate the mixture for 30 minutes.
4. Then create balls and roll in Parmesan cheese.

Nutritional Facts Per Serving
- Calories: 123
- Fat: 12.9 g
- Carb: 3 g
- Protein: 4.3 g

Pork Belly Fat Bombs

Prep time: 40 minutes /**Cooking time:** 0 minute/**Servings:** 6

Ingredients
- Bacon – 3 slices, cut in half widthwise
- Pork belly – 5.3 oz., cooked
- Mayonnaise – ¼ cup
- Dijon mustard – 1 Tbsp.
- Fresh horseradish – 1 Tbsp. grated
- Salt and pepper to taste
- Lettuce leaves – 6, for serving

Method
1. Preheat the oven to 325°F.
2. Cook the bacon slices in the oven on a baking sheet for 30 minutes. Let cool.
3. Crumble the bacon into a dish and set aside.

4. Shred the pork belly into a bowl. Mix in the horseradish, mustard, and mayonnaise. Season with salt and pepper.
5. Divide the mixture into 6 mounds.
6. Top with crumbled bacon and serve on top of lettuce leaves.

Nutritional Facts Per Serving
- Calories: 263
- Fat: 26.4 g
- Carb: 0.3 g
- Protein: 3.5 g

Veggie and Cheese Fat Bombs

Prep time: **45 minutes** /Cooking time: **6 minutes/**Servings:**6**

Ingredients

- Full-fat cream cheese – 3.5 oz.
- Unsalted butter – ¼ cup
- Ghee - 1 Tbsp.
- Onion – ½, chopped
- Garlic -1 clove, chopped
- Dried porcini mushrooms – ½ cup, chopped
- Spinach – 2 cups
- Salt and pepper to taste
- Hard goat cheese – ¼ cup, grated

Method

1. Mix the butter and cream cheese in a food processor.
2. Cook the onion and garlic with ghee in a frying pan for 3 minutes.
3. Add the spinach and chopped mushrooms. Cook for another 3 minutes. Set aside to cool.
4. Mix the butter-cream cheese mixture with the cooled spinach-mushroom mixture. Season with salt and pepper. Refrigerate for 30 minutes.
5. Make 5 balls out of the mixture.
6. Roll each ball in the goat cheese.
7. Serve.

Nutritional Facts Per Serving

- Calories: 166
- Fat: 16.7 g
- Carb: 3 g
- Protein: 3.4 g

Avocado, Macadamia, and Prosciutto Fat Bombs

Prep time: 7 minutes /**Cooking time:** 0 minute/**Servings:** 6

Ingredients
- Macadamia nuts – 4 oz.
- Avocado pulp – 4 oz.
- Cooked prosciutto – 1 oz., crumbled
- Freshly ground black pepper – ¼ tsp.

Method
1. Pulse macadamia nuts in a food processor until evenly crumbled. Divided in half.
2. In a bowl, combine half the macadamia nuts, avocado, crumbled prosciutto, and pepper. Mix.

3. Form mixture into 6 balls.
4. Place remaining crumbled macadamia nuts on a plate and roll balls in it to coat.
5. Serve.

Nutritional Facts Per Serving
- Calories: 170
- Fat: 17 g
- Carb: 2 g
- Protein: 3 g

Bacon Maple Pancake Balls

Prep time: **10 minutes** /Cook time: **0 minute**/Servings: **6**

Ingredients
- Bacon – 3 oz., cooked and chopped
- Cream cheese – 3 oz.
- Maple favoring – ½ tsp.
- Salt – ¼ tsp.
- Crushed pecans – 3 Tbsp.

Method

1. Combine bacon, cream cheese, maple flavoring, and salt in a bowl. Mix well.
2. Form mixture into 6 balls.

3. Place crushed pecans on a plate and roll balls in it to coat well.
4. Serve.

Nutritional Facts Per Serving
- Calories: 148
- Fat: 13 g
- Carb: 1 g
- Protein: 6 g

Barbecue Balls

Prep time: 2 hours 5 minutes /**Cooking time:** 0 minute /**Servings:** 6

Ingredients
- Cream cheese – 4 oz.
- Bacon fat – 4 Tbsp.
- Smoke flavoring – ½ tsp.
- Stevia – 2 drops
- Apple cider vinegar – ⅛ tsp.
- Sweet smoked chili powder – 1 Tbsp.
- Barbecue sauce – 3 Tbsp.

Method

1. In a food processor, combine all the ingredients except chili powder. Pulse until smooth and creamy, about 30 seconds.
2. Transfer mixture to a bowl and refrigerate for 2 hours.
3. Form the mixture into 6 balls.
4. Sprinkle balls with chili powder, rolling them around to coat all sides.
5. Pour barbecue sauce over balls.
6. Serve.

Nutritional Facts Per Serving
- Calories: 154
- Fat: 13 g
- Carb: 1 g
- Protein: 3 g

Conclusion

Fat Bombs are filling. They are low-carb snacks and packed with healthy fats and proteins. This book includes tried and tested fat bomb recipes that will help promote weight loss, increase energy, satisfy cravings and suppress hunger pangs. This Keto Fat Bombs Cookbook will teach you how to get perfect Fat Bombs every single time using only Keto approved ingredients.

www.ingramcontent.com/pod-product-compliance
Lightning Source LLC
Chambersburg PA
CBHW071437070526
44578CB00001B/113